Original title:
Golden Lights and Serene Nights

Copyright © 2025 Creative Arts Management OÜ
All rights reserved.

Author: Christian Leclair
ISBN HARDBACK: 978-3-69081-185-9
ISBN PAPERBACK: 978-3-69081-681-6

Aura of the Pastel Horizon

In the sky, a pink parade,
Marshmallow clouds twirl and sway,
The sun winks with a cheeky grin,
As daydreams dance to twilight's play.

Silly stars find their groove,
Skating on a moonbeam slide,
They giggle as the night unfolds,
Playing hide and seek with pride.

A raccoon dons a tiny hat,
While owls hoot in laughter's call,
Wind whispers jokes to shaking trees,
Foliage chuckles, it's a ball!

With every shade of laughter bright,
The world spins in joyful twirl,
In this realm of pastel hues,
Nonsense reigns, come join the whirl!

Shimmering Canopy Above

Stars are winking, oh so bright,
They giggle softly through the night.
A blanket tossed with sparkly thread,
While crickets dance, then go to bed.

A moonbeam peeks, with cheeky grin,
And whispers secrets, let's begin!
Each twist and turn, a cosmic prank,
As owls exchange their midnight thanks.

Nocturnal Glow and Silvery Streams

A firefly flips, he's quite the clown,
Bobbing about, can't keep him down!
He's got the moves, but not the beat,
With each little zap, he's on his feet.

The silver brook starts to hum along,
As fishes giggle in the song.
Each ripple hops, a splash of fun,
In this glow party, we've just begun!

Serenity Wrapped in Luminescence

Moonlight tickles the tips of trees,
While shadows play, a gently tease.
A slumbering bear with its sleepy snores,
Is dreaming of snacks, oh, the indoor scores!

The nightingale croons a silly tune,
While stars throw confetti, a jazzy boon.
A tranquil tune but laughter spreads,
As all of nature snickers in beds.

Flickering Lanterns on the Path

Lanterns flicker, a silly dance,
As shadows play, they take a chance.
A hedgehog rolls, mistaken for light,
And giggles erupt, what a sight!

The path ahead giggles with glee,
As crickets form a band, can't you see?
Each tiny glow is a friend for sure,
In this evening jaunt, who needs more?

Soft Echoes of Light's Departure

The sun slips away with a grin,
While squirrels in pajamas begin.
They dance in the dusk, quite a scene,
Beneath a sky that's turning green.

A cat on the fence gives a meow,
As fireflies gather, taking a bow.
The neighbors are laughing, what a sight,
As dusk brings out each wild delight.

Tender Murmurs of Twilight's Bliss

The moon pokes her head through the trees,
While crickets compose the night's easy symphonies.
A frog in a tux sings a tune,
While rabbits dance under the brightening moon.

Stars twinkle in a cheeky parade,
As shadows and giggles happily invade.
A frosty treat melts on my lap,
As the night winks with a friendly clap.

The Serenity of Dimming Horizons

The light takes a sip, then softly fades,
While bashful clouds wear their evening grades.
A hedgehog rolls by with a fumble,
While the sky chuckles, no need to grumble.

In twilight's embrace, toes wiggle in grass,
As fireflies flirt, their glow's such a sass.
Laughter erupts from a nearby scene,
As evening delights in moments unseen.

In the Glow of a Whispering Flame

A candle flickers in a playful breeze,
While marshmallows toast with endearing ease.
The laughter ignites with each funny tale,
And the night swells with giggles, a bright derail.

Bugs dance around in their tiny ball,
As I trip over logs and stumble, I fall.
The flame gives a wink, 'You're doing just fine,'
As we roast each other like the snacks on the line.

Celestial Glow on Softest Waves

Stars flicker like fireflies,
Mischief in the quiet skies.
A dolphin sings a silly tune,
While clams disco dance by the moon.

Seaweed twirls in the salty breeze,
Jellyfish wearing hats of cheese.
The moon chuckles, don't you see?
As waves splash in pure glee!

Crabs joke with the passing tides,
With pinching jokes and silly slides.
Glowworms light a wiggly parade,
In a world where laughter won't fade.

So join the fun beneath the beams,
Where night is filled with silly dreams.
Let the ocean's giggle take you far,
As we dance beneath the wispy stars.

Kisses of Light in the Midnight Air

Fireflies play hide and seek,
Their tiny dance is quite unique.
A raccoon wears a shiny crown,
While owls hoot their silly clown.

Cotton candy clouds above,
Whisper secrets like a dove.
A squirrel slides down a bright ray,
And giggles about his funny day.

Stars are winking bold and bright,
Sharing jokes in the soft night light.
A pancake moon flips in delight,
As critters laugh with all their might.

Join the laughter in the dark,
Let your heart ignite a spark.
With kisses from the twilight's hue,
Even shadows laugh with you!

Whispered Dreams in the Moon's Embrace

Hares wear pajamas to stargaze,
Dreaming up their funny ways.
While owls recite a bedtime tale,
With echoes of laughter on the trail.

Moonbeams tickle the slumbering trees,
As crickets laugh with quite the ease.
A fox juggles acorns with glee,
While the night air echoes their spree.

Cotton candy clouds drift by,
Whisking dreams like a slice of pie.
Shooting stars crash in silly fights,
Causing giggles in the quiet nights.

So lay down a blanket, join the dance,
As the dark invites you to take a chance.
For in the moon's sweet warm embrace,
Laughter lifts you to a joyful place.

A Tapestry of Light and Night

A snail in a bowtie slides along,
Singing the goofiest of songs.
While beetles tap their tiny feet,
In a concert that can't be beat.

The night fairies chuckle and play,
With twinkling lights in a bright array.
A tater tot rolls down the hill,
With laughter echoing, never still.

A porcupine contorts with glee,
Winking beneath a wild pine tree.
Light wraps around like a hug,
As critters dance with a funny shrug.

So come and join this silly night,
Where everything shines with pure delight.
In a tapestry woven of joy and fun,
Underneath the sleepy moonlit sun.

A Horizon Drenched in Fire

In the sky, a blaze so bright,
Chickens rush, it's almost night.
The sun's a comedian in disguise,
Juggling clouds and putting on ties.

Birds wear sunglasses, so cool and slick,
Chirping jokes, a funny trick.
The world laughs as shadows play,
Dancing with color, a wild ballet.

A squirrel slips on a branch so high,
Falling down, then gives a sigh.
"Oh dear sun, don't tease me so,
I'm here for nuts, not your show!"

As stars peek out with twinkling eyes,
The moon joins in, a starry guise.
They all gather for the evening fun,
Belly-laughing until the day is done.

Celestial Caress of Twilight

As day slips in a silky gown,
The squirrels giggle, wearing frowns.
Moonbeams tickle the tops of trees,
While shadows tease the buzzing bees.

The stars come out, a dazzling crew,
Playing cards with each passing hue.
The owls hoot, making snide remarks,
Telling stories of mischievous larks.

A raccoon dances on a fence,
Wobbling like it's got no sense.
"Why walk straight?" it seems to say,
"Life's a waltz, let's sway and sway!"

Fireflies flash, wearing tiny hats,
Sparking joy with their gentle chats.
As laughter floats on evening's breath,
They all embrace the night's sweet jest.

The Last Light's Whisper

The sun waves goodbye, a cheeky grin,
To crickets singing a silly din.
"Don't leave yet!" they croon and plead,
"We're still on the very first seed!"

The trees gossip, their branches sway,
Sharing secrets of the day's ballet.
"Did you see that rabbit's jump?
It looked like it fell in a big old lump!"

A cat with shades lounges on a fence,
Critiquing clouds—it's just common sense.
"Too puffy! They'll lose form and style,
I'll model for them, it's all worthwhile."

As evening drapes a velvet sheet,
The night giggles, teasing its feet.
The moon whispers, "Time for a laugh,
Let's tell tales of the day's silly gaff!"

Embraced by Evening's Calm

Twilight's curtain falls with flair,
Bats wear capes, zooming through the air.
Laughter echoes from a distant brook,
While skunks in tuxedos strike a look.

A hedgehog rolls, a spiky ball,
"Look at me, I could win it all!"
Dancing through daisies with style and grace,
Waddling off, it's a hilarious race.

Crickets cheer as shadows creep,
While daisies giggle, they can't help but leap.
The moon winks down with a teasing glow,
"Let's see who dances, come on, put on a show!"

The night hums soft, a merry tune,
As fireflies twirl, under the moon.
With smiles bright, and hearts set free,
The world's a comedy, just you and me.

Reflections of a Fading Sun

The sun wears a hat, oh what a sight,
Its rays dance around, not shy but polite.
It brushes the clouds with a wink and a grin,
As shadows grow longer, let the fun begin.

The birds hold a meeting, on branches they sit,
Debating the best way to land, what a hit!
With every loud tweet, they decide on a plan,
Only to take flight, each one like a fan.

Harmony in the Hushed Hours

The moon hums a tune, slightly off-key,
While owls hoot along with a cup of green tea.
Stars twinkle in time, not always aligned,
As crickets snap fingers, oh won't you unwind!

A raccoon with style, in a bow tie he roams,
Searching for snacks, his favorite dimes and bones.
He winks at the night, with mischief in mind,
As fireflies join in, all feeling quite fine.

The Constellation's Promise

The Big Dipper spills tea, what a thrilling affair,
While Orion shows up in his faux furry wear.
The stars gossip loudly, about last night's dance,
While comets zip by, offering a chance.

With patterns so wacky, what stories they share,
Like Venus in sneakers, unaware of her glare.
A cosmic debate, who shines the most bright,
While the Milky Way grins, staying out of sight.

Twilight's Golden Embrace

As twilight arrives, the snacks hit the scene,
Peanut butter sandwiches, the twilight cuisine.
Fire pits flicker, and laughter takes flight,
While the stars throw a party, how silly the night!

A squirrel in a tutu, quite ready to prance,
Joins fireflies twirling in a whimsy dance.
Around marshmallow clouds, they'd dodge and they'd spin,
While the moon giggles softly, inviting new kin.

Day's End Reverie

As the sun takes a bow, what a sight,
The clouds wear pink, the world feels light.
A dance of shadows, a silly parade,
Even the squirrels seem to masquerade.

With ice cream drips and laughter galore,
The neighbor's cat plays with a sock on the floor.
Fireflies flicker like tiny fireworks,
While all the dogs conspire with their quirks.

The moon peeks out, gives a wink so sly,
A jaybird squawks a joke, oh my, oh my!
The day's silliness now takes its throne,
Under a sky that's gently overblown.

Cheers to weirdness, celebrate the fade,
Nighttime's a canvas where laughter's laid.
With sleepy giggles and whimsical dreams,
Who knew that dusk would unravel such themes?

Basked in Amber Hues

The sun is melting like a gooey treat,
Whipped cream clouds swirl, it's hard to compete.
Bicycles wobble in the heat of the glow,
While ants in their suits have a parade to show.

A breeze brings whispers, a ticklish affair,
It steals my hat, making me swear,
I chase it down, oh what a scene,
A cartoon moment that's quite unforeseen.

As shadows stretch like lazy cats,
Nearby, a raccoon dons some stylish hats.
It's a gathering of critters in party mode,
Each with a snack, including popcorn stowed.

Even the stars giggle as they peep,
Jokes on the moon, "Are you counting sheep?"
Twinkling like chandeliers in a roast,
Laughter's the spirit we cherish the most.

The Quietude of Nocturnal Bliss

The crickets tune up, it's a motley crew,
While owls debate who's the wisest, it's true.
A hedgehog rolls by, brave and round,
In a night-time stroll, mystery found.

With cookies crumbling near a soft lamp's glow,
A raccoon sneaks by, moves incredibly slow.
Each rustle inviting a curious gaze,
It's giggle-worthy amidst the night's haze.

The moon laughs softly at the world below,
It's a cosmic soap opera, a grand show.
With blankets of stars stitching stories tight,
The night wears laughter like a sparkly light.

Grandma's snoring adds to the scene,
While shadows prance like they've never been keen.
In this nocturnal symphony, we find delight,
Who knew that silence could feel so bright?

Echoes of Dimming Light

As the light starts to fade, a clown takes the stage,
Wearing socks two different colors, oh what a rage!
The bushes whisper secrets only they know,
While the sun's cheeky grin begins to bestow.

Balloons drift by, playing tag with the trees,
A dog chases shadows, saying "Hey, please!"
The world spins around like it's lost in a dance,
With laughter and hiccups, we take our chance.

In the twilight's embrace, the snacks come alive,
Cookies and chips in a hilarious hive.
The stars pop out, like they're bursting to laugh,
They twinkle in rhythm, as we draw a path.

So here's to the moments that tickle our souls,
As day turns to night, we stay in our roles.
Witty banter floats like confetti in flight,
In shadows and giggles, we revel in light.

The Radiant Horizon

A chicken danced on the hilltop,
Hens watched with beaks agape.
The sky blushed pink for a moment,
While cows tried to escape.

The sun wore silly sunglasses,
Beaming like a goofball bright.
Clouds were laughing in the background,
As day traded spots with night.

A dog howled at a passing star,
A cat snored loud, count sheep.
With all this fun and frolic,
Who needs the bliss of sleep?

So let's toast to this madness,
With lemonade and a cheer.
Here's to the silly moments,
That bring us all such queer!

Lullabies of the Sun

The sun decided to play peekaboo,
Hiding behind a big ol' hat.
Bunnies giggled in the meadow,
While squirrels argued about the cat.

A wise owl sang a tune,
That made the crickets dance.
But bees were too busy buzzing,
To even take a chance.

Fireflies dressed up like fairies,
Twinkling with a wink and grin.
The whole scene felt like a party,
And nobody wanted to pin.

So as the day slips away,
And night brings its delightful lure,
Let's laugh at the day gone by,
And whisper deeds that stir!

Liquid Gold at Sundown

The sun spilled juice on the horizon,
As if it were too much to hold.
Fish were laughing up in the stream,
While turtles tried to be bold.

Pigs were rolling in the mud,
Giggling as they twirled.
With crowns made of dandelions,
They claimed this wacky world.

A disco ball hung from a branch,
Reflecting colors so rare.
The wind joined in with a shimmy,
Causing butterflies to stare.

So let's raise our cups to the sunset,
To moments that make us grin.
For laughter is the best recipe,
A sweet joy we can always win!

Tranquil Reflections

The moon wore a cozy sweater,
As stars danced with delight.
Crickets held a talent show,
With their chirpings through the night.

A bear decided to juggle,
While frogs croaked their loud tune.
Even shadows were laughing,
Under the watchful moon.

The night air smelled of popcorn,
As fireflies put on a play.
Mysteries of night unfurling,
In their own silly way.

So grab your friends and join the fun,
In the waltz of the night.
For even when the world is dark,
We find joy in the light!

Nightfall's Gentle Glow

As the sun starts to snore,
The moon plays peek-a-boo.
Bats make silly faces,
While crickets sing a tune.

Fireflies dance like mad,
In the twilight's warm embrace.
They flicker, blink, and twirl,
Like they've won a silly race.

Clouds fluff up like pillows,
Resting from their drifting spree.
The cats chase after shadows,
Thinking it's a game of freeze.

Laughter floats on cool breezes,
While owls hoot in delight.
What a whimsical universe,
In the charm of the night!

The Warmth of Dimming Days

When the sun decides to nap,
The sky wears a sleepy grin.
Squirrels toast their nuts,
With hats made from old tin.

Tea parties on the lawn,
Ants bring crumbs like fine bread.
Grasshoppers try to tango,
While beetles form a band instead.

The horizon paints itself,
With colors all askew.
It's a wild mix of chaos,
Like a toddler with a glue.

As twilight spins its yarn,
The shadows wink and sway.
A chorus of mischief sings,
It's a jolly twilight play!

A Canvas of Celestial Colors

Brushstrokes of pink and purple,
Splatter on the canvas blue.
Stars giggle at the painters,
Who've spilled more than a few.

A comet takes a selfie,
Catch it quick before it fades!
The milky way is grinning,
With all its shining parades.

The clouds wear shades of orange,
Like they're off to a show.
It's a party in the heavens,
Everyone needs to know!

Fireworks pop in laughter,
As night drapes its velvet sheet.
This cosmic jamboree of colors,
Is where silly dreams meet!

Stars Akimbo in the Night

Stars are all quite disheveled,
Sprinkled across the sky.
They twirl and dip like dancers,
With themes of a party high.

One star trips on a comet,
And falls in a tweet of gleam.
While others roll in laughter,
Creating their own starry scheme.

Planets gaze in wonder,
At the antics from the above.
Like kids in a playground,
They bounce in fun and love.

In the cool embrace of night,
All the lights share a wink.
With laughter echoing softly,
It's bliss, don't you think?

The Dawn's Embrace

The rooster crows with flair and glee,
His alarm clock's set for half past three.
The sun peeks in with a sleepy grin,
As cats play tags, oh where to begin?

Coffee spills like an artist's dream,
While squirrels plot a daring scheme.
With toast that jumps, oh what a sight,
Mornings spark joy—such pure delight!

Pajamas dance, the socks take flight,
As dreams collide with morning light.
With sleepy yawns and mismatched shoes,
We greet the day, no time to snooze!

So raise a mug, let's start this race,
In the happy chaos, find your place!
Life's a circus, with twists so tight,
Embrace the fun in morning's light!

Whispers of Twilight

As shadows stretch, the laughter flows,
In cozy warmth, the mischief grows.
A moonlit dance on the garden path,
Where gnomes giggle and embrace their math.

Fireflies glow, like tiny stars,
While crickets play their funny guitars.
With picnic pies that take a dive,
We chase the snacks that seem alive!

The shadows talk, with playful hiss,
Of sneaky ghosts and twilight bliss.
With whispers soft, they share a jest,
In twilight's arms, we find our best.

So gather 'round as night takes flight,
In the magic of fading light.
With laughter rich and hearts so bright,
The evening hums and feels just right!

Radiance at Dusk

The sun dips low with a golden pout,
While ducks debate on a route to shout.
Clouds wear pink, a fashion scene,
As squirrels fight over a berry queen!

Bikes zoom by with a wheeled delight,
As friends slip in for a lazy night.
With pizza boxes and soda cans,
We feast like kings, ignoring plans!

The stars peek out, all crisp and neat,
While shadows battle for prime seats.
With giggles echoing through the dusk,
This joyful chaos is a must!

So raise your glasses, toast the sun,
For every dusk brings more fun.
As laughter echoes, and worries fade,
In radiant hues, memories are made!

A Symphony of Shadows

The night unfolds like a giant book,
Where mischief brews in every nook.
With owls wearing glasses, wise and round,
The secrets of the forest abound!

Crickets tune up for a serenade,
While creatures play in the cool glade.
As laughter lingers in the chill,
Each shadow spins with a humorous thrill!

Dancing branches, twirling leaves,
In a comedy where nature weaves.
With fireflies joining the lively tune,
The night is bright, as dreams attune!

So kick your shoes and join the dance,
In shadows where the funny prance.
A symphony played under the stars,
With giggles echoing near and far!

Traces of Serenity Across the Sea

A crab waltzes in disguise,
With shells as shades of pies.
Jellyfish dance with jellybeans,
Making waves in silly scenes.

Seagulls squawk a funny tune,
Winking at the rising moon.
Fish wear hats and bow ties too,
While dolphins break into a crew.

Tides tickle sandcastles made,
As giggles rise with each cascade.
The sunset paints the surf with glee,
A comic show across the sea.

As soft waves sing their playful song,
We laugh at fish that swim along.
With every splash, a joke is told,
In waters warm that never grow old.

Flickers of Bliss Under Moonbeams

Fireflies twinkle with delight,
Competing with stars on this balmy night.
A raccoon dons a fancy scarf,
While crickets chirp a silly arf!

In the garden, shadows prance,
As flowers join in on the dance.
Night owls hoot, then crack a pun,
As bats perform—oh, what fun!

The moon smirks, a cheeky glow,
As hedgehogs roll in a line, oh so slow.
With each flicker, the laughter flows,
In this nighttime show, anything goes!

Underneath the sky so vast,
Time tickles by, our worries past.
With jokes and jests floating free,
This is joy, can't you see?

Lullabies of the Fading Sun

As the sun bows down with grace,
A turtle races, but in slow pace.
Bumblebees yawn and stretch their legs,
While ladybugs trade tiny pegs.

Colors swirl, painting the air,
A snail joins in with style and flair.
The breeze tells tales of strange delights,
While shadows stretch and tickle sights.

Squirrels giggle as nuts take flight,
Making twilight their joyful night.
With every brightening star, they cheer,
For laughter's ring is always near.

As day bids farewell with a wink,
Creatures gather to hug and think.
The night hugs them, and all is bright,
In lullabies of fading light.

Soft Reflections in Dusky Waters

Ripples giggle, a playful scene,
A frog wears spectacles, oh so keen.
Tadpoles twirl in a dance of dreams,
While shadows create funny schemes.

Pebbles throw wishes at the moon,
A fish sings a jazzy tune.
Leaves rustle, whispering jokes anew,
As the wind joins in, laughing too.

With each splash, a new giggle is born,
Reeds sway gently, the night is adorned.
The sky chuckles, stars drop down,
Making puddles smooth and brown.

Every ripple reflects the cheer,
As night creatures gather near.
In dusky waters, joy takes flight,
Where laughter echoes long into the night.

Evening's Harmonious Glow

As the sun sets with a wink,
The crickets start their tunes to think.
Fireflies perform their glowing dance,
While I trip on my own small pants.

The stars take stage, a laugh or two,
My neighbor's cat thinks it's a zoo.
Laughter spreads through the twilight air,
Just watch out for the rogue pizza share.

Under sky filled with twinkling cheer,
I shout to the moon, 'Hey, lend me your beer!'
The clouds blush pink with whispers bright,
While dogs howl their own comedic plight.

The night rolls on, a playful tide,
As moths play tag, and I try to hide.
With each laugh and giggle, sparks ignite,
Best not trip while dancing in the light.

The Soft Embrace of Amber Hours

Orange hues paint the evening sea,
A raccoon steals my snacks with glee.
The world's a stage, the stars our mates,
While I bumble 'round with my awkward fates.

A breeze whispers jokes from afar,
My dog sneezes, it's the funniest star.
Lawn chairs creak like an old man's knee,
As I attempt yoga—oh, let me be!

Giggling owls hold their sides with glee,
They roll their eyes at my antics, you see.
The moon chuckles at my fashion spree,
Wishing I'd just wear a simple tee.

But no, I strut in my neon glow,
Making friends with the night, just so you know.
As laughter echoes, the fun never ends,
This comedy show is for magical friends.

Twilight's Gentle Promise

The sky dons a hat of soft twilight,
As squirrels debate if it's time for a bite.
They chatter away, full of wise cracking,
While I trip over roots and start laughing.

Shadows stretch like lazy cats,
Neighborhood kids have grand ol' chats.
Fires crackle with stories and jokes,
While I mix up desserts with my toasts.

Stars blink in, curious about the show,
I juggle hot dogs; oh no, now they glow!
The moon rolls its eyes at my silly plight,
Inviting all to join the night's delight.

With every chuckle, spirits rise high,
As crickets chirp like they're on the fly.
Twilight's canvas becomes our stage,
Each pun we share is a new playful page.

The Dawn of Stardust Moments

As dawn creeps in, the world seems bold,
A rooster crows, but it's slightly cold.
The sun peeks over, giving a wink,
While I fumble about, eyeing my drink.

The coffee spills with a comical splash,
I laugh at the cat, oh, he's such a brash.
Breakfast becomes a circus delight,
As eggs try to dance like they're out of sight.

Birds perform their morning tunes,
While I join in, bemused by my goons.
The pancakes flip and fly with flair,
A true breakfast skit—a chaotic affair!

So here's to the moments of pure, silly bliss,
In the sparkle of dawn, no chance we'll miss.
With laughter and sunbeams, we begin anew,
In this dance of humor, life feels askew.

Radiance in the Twilight

As the daylight starts to fade,
The frogs begin their serenade.
Stars appear with silly grins,
While shadows dance in leafy skins.

A cat proclaims its royal right,
To rule the yard in waning light.
Fireflies twirl like tiny planes,
As crickets join in happy strains.

The moon sneaks in, a sly old fox,
Replacing clocks with silly knocks.
Laughing clouds play hide and seek,
While owls discuss the day of the week.

So let the twilight bring its cheer,
With creatures popping out, oh dear!
A world where giggles take their flight,
In the whimsical glow of the night.

Luminous Whispers at Dusk

In twilight's soft and giggly glow,
A squirrel juggles nuts, you know.
The moon winks down, a friendly tease,
As shadows frolic in the breeze.

Bats swoop low, a flying band,
With antics we can't understand.
They wiggle and they wobble tight,
Making mischief with delight.

The stars all twinkle, sharing jokes,
While rabbits laugh in silly cloaks.
"Why did the chicken cross the road?"
Under starlit giggles, new tales are sowed.

So gather round as day departs,
With joyful sounds in cheerful hearts.
The night, it seems, just loves to play,
In the glow where laughter holds sway.

Echoes of the Setting Sun

The sun dips low, a cheeky grin,
While birds burst forth in frothy spin.
They flap and squawk, a silly crew,
As dusk paints skies in different hues.

Laughter bubbles in the air,
With fireflies dancing everywhere.
Crickets chirp a rhythmic plight,
In the shimmery sound of night.

A dog gives chase to his own tail,
As confused cats begin to wail.
In the twilight, fun takes flight,
Where every moment feels just right.

So raise a glass to skies that gleam,
As stars giggle and moonbeams beam.
In echoes of a playful sun,
The night is here; let's have some fun!

A Symphony of Starlit Hues

A quirky symphony fills the air,
With frogs in tuxedos, bold and rare.
They croak the notes, a vibrant tune,
While owls conduct beneath the moon.

The sky's a canvas, splashed with glee,
As fireflies dance in harmony.
Whispers of joy and laughs unite,
In this colorful, silly night.

Each twinkling star has tales to share,
Of mischief and fun, beyond compare.
As shadows join the playful beat,
And giggles echo on the street.

So grab your friends to join the spree,
With laughter as our melody.
In the symphony of starlit hues,
The night unfolds with joyful views.

Hues of Tranquil Twilight

The sky blushes pink, a squirrel sings,
While a cat plots mischief with imagined wings.
A dog barks loudly, lost in a chase,
Chasing shadows in a twilight embrace.

Chairs rock slowly, a breeze whispers bold,
As ants march in line, their secrets unfold.
A leaf falls down with a comical twist,
This peaceful scene wrapped in sunset's mist.

A frog croaks loudly, a cringe-worthy tune,
Jumping around like they've lost their maroon.
The stars peek out, a twinkle so sly,
In this surreal moment, we giggle and sigh.

Nature turns silly, as light starts to fade,
In this quirky wonder, no plans to invade.
With chuckles and grins, we relish the show,
As daylight departs, the fun starts to grow.

Illuminated Dreams on Horizon's Edge

The world's aglow with a quirky charm,
As shadows play tricks, they mean no harm.
A raccoon in shades, with suave little moves,
Dances at dusk, making up groovy grooves.

A tweet from a bird, a rhyming surprise,
While the moon just chuckles, oh how it flies.
A breeze carries laughter, tickling our ears,
Like a funny joke shared over many beers.

With fireflies flickering, like tiny disco balls,
We laugh with the crickets in their call-and-response brawls.
Nature's a comedian, cracking up the night,
As we stretch on the grass, all feels just right.

The horizon dips low, in a humorous spin,
Where dreams weave in jest, with a wide, toothy grin.
We won't take it serious, why worry or fret?
In this dreamland of fun, we'll double our bets.

A Dance of Fireflies in the Dark

Tiny lights flicker, like stars that have legs,
With all the enthusiasm of playful little pegs.
They swirl and they twirl, oh what a delight,
Beaming with joy in the still of the night.

A gang of them giggles, while flashing their art,
They weave through tall grass, the night's little heart.
Each flicker a wink, each dance like a game,
In this laughter-filled space, nothing feels tame.

A nearby frog croaks, keeps time with the show,
In its jumpy little ways, oh, how we all glow!
As the darkness giggles, the moon gives a sigh,
With a chuckle, it winks, "Let's give this a try."

While we watch in awe, bursting with cheer,
The night comes alive, full of whimsy, my dear.
With fireflies leading us, twinkling sparks soar,
In this silly dance party, who could ask for more?

The Warmth of Dusk's Last Breath

A warm hug descends as the sun says farewell,
With giggles and whispers that tumble and swell.
The shadows all grow, playing peek-a-boo games,
As everyone laughs, calling out silly names.

The swing set is creaking, a ghost in disguise,
But it's just old Gary, with mischievous eyes.
He swings to the rhythm of dusk's giddy beat,
Chasing away worries with each playful feat.

The chill of the night brings sweaters and laughs,
As stars start to wink like mischievous staffs.
The world all aglow with this lighthearted cheer,
With each passing moment, we cherish the near.

As night spreads its wings, we snuggle up tight,
In this cozy cocoon, everything feels right.
With laughter and warmth, we savor these hours,
In the embrace of the dusk, we bloom like bright flowers.

Reflections of Light on Water's Edge

Ripples ripple, splashing sounds,
Frogs in chorus, quite the clowns.
A duck in dance, a swan in jest,
　Mirror, mirror, who's the best?

In the night, the moon is winking,
While fish debate what they're thinking.
Stars above are dropping snacks,
Splashing fish—let's call it pranks.

With a jig, a jig, they glide along,
　Making waves, a watery song.
Laughter bounces off the shore,
　"Is that a splash or just a snore?"

Sleepy sun, take your leave,
Frogs are here, you wouldn't believe!
Water's edge, a stage set right,
For wacky plays in cool moonlight.

Starlit Corridor of Wishes

Under the sky—a flurry of dreams,
Twinkling stars in whimsical schemes.
Wish upon a comet made of cheese,
  Find a dream that aims to please!

Down the path of glitter and glee,
  Noses twitching, a rabbit decree.
Laughter echoes, let's be merry,
With every hop, the jokes get scary!

A squirrel pauses with a quirky grin,
"I saw a wish that snuck right in!"
The moon laughs, a beam of light,
As umbrellas pop in the night's delight.

Join the dance, as wishes collide,
  With silly dreams we cannot hide.
Through the corridor, endlessly bright,
  Each step a giggle, oh what a sight!

Embracing the Whispering Glow

Balloons float, the night is young,
A breeze whispers of tales unsung.
Fireflies tinkle, a blink of light,
"Catch me if you can!" they ignite the night.

With a hop, the shadows play,
In a game where no one can stay.
A cactus chuckles, brimming with cheer,
"Why not bring snacks for all right here?"

Glowing friends in every hue,
Crafting laughs and stories too.
Under the canopy, all's aglow,
"Dance like nobody's watching!" we bestow.

Time stands still when giggles zoom,
As we gather 'round the lighted room.
Embrace the squishy spark of night,
In a world where whimsy takes flight!

The Last Rays of Day's Tender Hand

As the sun bows, a funny twist,
Daytime stories can't be missed.
Crickets chirp on a variety show,
"What's your best joke?" they steal the glow!

A squirrel struts, a crown of leaves,
"Why did I climb? For more fun, geez!"
Light drips down on a dancing snail,
With a beat, slowly escaping the trail.

Fuzzy shadows hop and glide,
In the dance of dusk, where critters bide.
With every giggle, the night expands,
As the last rays tickle, soft in hands.

Hold tight to smiles, for laughter's free,
In this zany show of night's decree.
So let's prance into the sudden dark,
Where laughter glows like a lovely spark!

Moonlight Serenade

The moon danced bright in the sky,
With stars winking as they passed by.
A raccoon wore shades, thought he was cool,
While fireflies twinkled, a glowing fool.

The crickets croaked a symphony,
One sang off-key, just for the spree.
Owls hooted laughs, their feathers a mess,
While hedgehogs rolled by in their evening dress.

The breeze whispered jokes in the trees,
Telling tales that tickled the knees.
A deer tried to moonwalk, slipped on some grass,
And all of us giggled, as good times amassed.

As night wore on, the fun never ceased,
With laughter and frolic, we felt quite pleased.
For under the moon's charming gaze,
Life was a party with whimsical ways.

Glimmers of Hope

Fireflies buzzing in a happy parade,
While mice held their picnic on a leaf glade.
A raccoon in a tux, tipping his hat,
Said, "Join my party, we'll dine on some fat!"

A squirrel juggled acorns without a care,
While rabbits played hopscotch, a funny affair.
The owls dropped in, with snacks to share,
But their jokes were so corny, we couldn't bear.

The moonlight shone on a cheery dance mat,
With turtles in top hats, how about that!
They spun and they twirled, their shells all aglow,
While the grasshoppers cheered from their front row.

As the night went on, we snickered and sighed,
For in this odd world, our dreams could collide.
With laughter our compass, we found our delight,
Chasing glimmers of joy in the still of the night.

Evening's Soft Caress

Evening breezes tickle my nose,
As a cat dreams of catching a garden hose.
The stars laughed, blinked with sheer delight,
While a frog croaked jokes about the moonlight.

A dog in pajamas snoozed by the tree,
Counting the flavors of honeyed brie.
The clouds were marshmallows drifting afar,
While crickets were busy tuning their guitar.

A fox strummed softly, singing a tune,
To woo a raccoon under a silver balloon.
They shared silly stories of past nighttime blunders,
As bat's entertained with acrobatic wonders.

The sway of the night held a giggling cheer,
As laughter echoed, so joyful and clear.
In this cozy chaos where fun took its rest,
We found evening's magic, a burst of zest.

Celestial Dreams Awaken

When stars are lit, and laughter flows,
The cats wear crowns, and anything goes.
A mouse rode a dog, just for a thrill,
While planets twirled, they all had their fill.

The moon flashed a grin as it switched on its beams,
While fireflies gathered for fluttery dreams.
A wise old owl told the best bedtime tale,
Of how squirrels once flew on a funky whale.

The night draped joy over all it could see,
While critters played charades under the tree.
Every rustle and chirp made the fun unite,
With giggles and grins in the soft starlight.

As we lay on the grass without a worry,
We danced with the clouds, all in a hurry.
In celestial corners where dreams are spun,
We found the odd charm of a humorous run.

Illuminated Paths of Serenity

In the glow of the moon's soft beam,
Cats prance in a whimsical dream.
A squirrel dances, oh what a sight,
As shadows play hide-and-seek tonight.

Balloons float by on a gentle breeze,
Tangled in branches, they tease the trees.
A dog barks softly, in playful cheer,
While the stars giggle, almost near.

Chasing fireflies with glee so bright,
Mice take cover, fearing the night.
Laughter echoes, the kids take flight,
As the moon winks, oh such a delight!

So let's embrace this merry parade,
Where jokes are made and spirits aren't swayed.
In the evening's embrace, we find our way,
With laughter and joy leading the fray.

The Charm of Nightly Radiance

A glow worm wears a tiny hat,
Sipping dew, oh what a brat!
Hopping around with a tiny grin,
While crickets join in with a din.

Baking cookies under starlit skies,
The oven's on fire, to our surprise!
Making wishes on a shooting star,
With cookie dough stuck, oh how bizarre!

A turtle races, oh what a feat,
With a rabbit, oh isn't that neat?
They call it a tie, how could this be?
In the night's charm, they're all carefree.

So dance with the shadows, shake off your care,
Share your stories, if you dare.
For with each glimmer and humorous plight,
The night rejuvenates, oh what a sight!

Glowing Echoes of Yesterday's Light

Remember the times when we could not stop?
With glow sticks and laughter, we'd dance at the top.
Mismatched socks, our outfit delight,
Twinkling like stars in the unending night.

Dandelion wishes swirl in the breeze,
Chasing the ranbows with absolute ease.
Scooters and skates, oh what a race,
With smiles painted wide across every face.

Old tales resound with a comedic twist,
As we delve into memories that can't be missed.
With each sentence that rolls off the tongue,
The laughter erupts, forever young.

So here's to the echoes that bounce and play,
In the depth of the night, they come out to stay.
Each giggle and grin, a beacon of cheer,
In the magical moments we all hold dear.

Secrets Shared in the Twilight Hour

Whispers float on the cool evening air,
As secrets unravel, we giggle and stare.
A raccoon spills tea on the porch's old chair,
While the owls wear glasses, pretending to care.

A flashlight thief sneaks around the block,
Shining on friends, what a funny shock!
Each beam a story, a chuckle adds cheer,
In the cozy dark, where all feels near.

S'mores are roasted, with laughter in swirls,
Pillow fights break out, as chaos unfurls.
The stars blink down, oh what a sight,
As we share our secrets, hidden from light.

So let's treasure this twilight, our goofy little clan,
With jokes shared in whispers, the joy will expand.
For in the embrace of the night's gentle power,
We find our joy in the twilight hour.

A Canvas of Quiet Light

In the sky, a pancake hangs,
Flipping soft, it calls my name,
Butterflies made of candy,
Dance around, driving me insane.

The stars wear hats, so bright and funny,
Glowing brightly, like a bunch of bunnies,
I asked the moon for a slice of pie,
He chuckled loud and said, 'Oh my!'

The clouds are pillows, soft and sweet,
Twirling like dancers on their feet,
I tried to sit, but it was a trick,
I bounced instead, it made me sick.

In this light, laughter fills the air,
A silly world, without a care,
As night unfolds its laughing charm,
I roll around, not a single harm.

Celestial Serenade Beyond the Horizon

The sky cracked jokes like a stand-up king,
  Stars giggled while the night took wing,
  A comet zoomed by with a zany grin,
  'Catch me if you can!' it dared to spin.

The moon wore shades, looking quite cool,
  Told the sun, 'You're a daytime fool!'
  While crickets chirped their silly tunes,
  The fireflies danced, a wobbly swoon.

  A shooting star fell right on my plate,
  I asked for fries — the wait was great!
  Sirius waggled its tail with glee,
  Saying, 'Wish wisely; order with me!'

  So I chuckled with each stellar friend,
  In this night where the fun won't end,
  A funny sky, a cosmic jest,
  I laughed out loud; it felt the best.

Reflections in the Quietude

A lake of giggles, smooth as glass,
Frogs in tuxedos make quite a splash,
The moon's reflection winked with cheer,
'Join us, friends! The laughs are here!'

A fish in bubbles sings pop tunes,
While turtles shuffle in silly cartoons,
I watched a duck do the moonwalk sway,
Quacking in rhythm as night turned to play.

I tossed pebbles, each made a joke,
Rippling laughter, an aquatic poke,
'You splash too hard!' the minnows yelled,
As pillows of clouds around me swelled.

Such fun reflections, soft and bright,
The calm of evening turned to delight,
I waved to the stars, a friendly sight,
As night unraveled in laughter's light.

Enchanted Glow of the Nightfall

The darkness tickled silly and loud,
With fireflies buzzing, gathering a crowd,
As night fell softly in sparkly sheets,
A parade of crickets danced on their feet.

Kites made of shadow swirled through the air,
'Caught you!' they giggled without a care,
The moon giggled and shared a rhyme,
Even the owls, feeling quite prime.

A raccoon's party, snacks all around,
They fed on laughter without a sound,
A dance with the twilight, a wacky spree,
As stars joined in, singing with glee.

Enchanting nights filled with whimsy and bliss,
Gave every moment a comical twist,
With each glowing spark, a joy takes flight,
In a magical realm where all feels right.

Moments that Dazzle in Moonlight

Under a sky where giggles bloom,
Cats wear hats in a scented room.
Jellybeans dance on the soft-cooked grass,
While owls in tuxedos invite folks to sass.

Fireflies play tag with the waning sun,
Bats in bow ties insist it's all in fun.
A snail in a vest claims he's quite the catch,
But only when the moon lights up the patch.

Crickets conduct with a zingy tune,
Mice in ballet shoes pirouette by the moon.
The night can be weird, a whimsical spree,
Where clowns paint their faces just to be free.

In this odd realm, joy does not cease,
Silly shadows waltz, lending a bit of peace.
Under the sparkles, laughter takes flight,
In moments like these, hearts feel just right.

The Allure of Night's Tender Glow

With a wink, the stars make a silly bet,
Who can sing louder—a crow or a pet?
Raccoons don sunglasses, strutting with flair,
Chasing shadows away without a care.

The moon hangs low, playing peek-a-boo,
Silly rabbits hop, munching on dew.
Jokes are cracked by a snickering breeze,
While turtles in slippers take it with ease.

Past midnight, squirrels gather in style,
Complaining the nuts were a little while.
Dancing with muffins, they twirl on the lawn,
As the fireflies giggle and flicker at dawn.

Every twinkle brings a chuckle and cheer,
In the calm of the night, fun's always near.
The allure of whimsy glows ever bright,
In laughter and dreams that take flight at night.

Silhouettes of Light in Subtle Shades

Dancing in shadows, a parade of bliss,
Chubby raccoons share a chipmunk's kiss.
In the twilight glow, they twirl and sway,
While crickets mark time with a sing-song play.

A fox dons a scarf, looking ever so fab,
While old socks become hats for the bubbly crab.
Whispers of giggles float soft on the stream,
As everyone joins in this odd, happy dream.

The moon's a comedian winking with glee,
While prancing through forests where bumblebees flee.
Stealing the spotlight, a tortoise runs late,
With tales of his travels that seem to elate.

In the silhouettes cast by a gentle light,
Even shadows wear smiles that shine through the night.
So raise a toast to this silly brigade,
Where laughter's the currency; joy is well paid.

The Sigh of Dusk's Gentle Caress

As dusk settles down, a sweet breath reveals,
A llama in sunglasses stealing some meals.
The trees sway gently, their branches do dance,
While owls make up stories that leave you in trance.

In cozy corners, popcorn pops high,
While hedgehogs debate how low they can fly.
The sigh of the night brings whimsical fright,
As shadows turn silly, embracing delight.

Frogs leap in tuxes, croaking their tunes,
Spinning soft tales 'neath the glimmering moons.
A picnic of giggles spreads wide on the ground,
Where laughter and joy merrily abound.

With every soft sigh from the dusk's embrace,
Mischief untangles, leaving giggles in place.
As the night whispers secrets and winks in retreat,
Chasing after chuckles feels bittersweet.

Glimmers in the Shadowed Sky

Stars blink in mischievous glee,
They dance with comets, wild and free.
A chicken worries up above,
Clucking dreams of cosmic love.

The moon wears a wobbly grin,
While asteroids dance, tossing pin.
A squirrel in a spaceship takes flight,
Chasing a squirrel, oh what a sight!

Neon beams of joy collide,
As meteors take a joyride.
Wishes whispered, quirky and spry,
Under the glimmers of the sky.

In this lunatic ball of night,
Everything feels just so right.
So grab your snacks, laugh out loud,
Join the cosmic, silly crowd!

Celestial Embers Embrace the Night

A firefly wears a tiny hat,
Calling wishes, 'How about that?'
The twinkling stars join in a race,
With wobbly moons in dizzy space.

A comet whoops, then takes a dive,
Juggling planets, oh what a vibe!
Galaxies giggle, colors so bright,
Creating chaos in the night.

Saturn spills rings of neon glow,
While Pluto plays peek-a-boo below.
Tickled by laughter that fills the air,
In this cosmic crazy fair.

See the meteors skip and bounce,
As laughter echoes, all astounds.
In this night where silliness roams,
All the stars feel right at home!

The Gilded Veil of Evening

The night swirls in a silly fray,
While shadows dance in a wobbly sway.
Crickets chirp a catchy tune,
That makes the fireflies hum in June.

A moonbeam trips, falls on a cat,
Who laughs and gives a startled 'what?'
Stars play tag with puffs of cloud,
Underneath a nighttime shroud.

Twilight whispers funny fables,
While the night unveils its tables.
Dinner with aliens? What a delight,
As they munch on stars, oh what a sight!

Laughter sparkles in the air,
As wishes flutter without a care.
In the evening's gilded delight,
We're all just kids in the moonlight!

Moonlit Reverie

The moon, a giant disco ball,
Reflecting giggles, hear them all.
Stars hum a tune, so delightfully sweet,
While the owls breakdance on their feet.

Bats wear shades, flapping in style,
Making the nighttime all worthwhile.
A raccoon joins with a joyful spin,
Searching for snacks — let the fun begin!

Galaxy marshmallows float through the sky,
While laughter tickles a passing sigh.
Planets play hopscotch in a line,
Creating games that are simply divine.

At night's outrageous, shimmering glow,
Where everything bounces and nothing is slow.
Join the frivolity, let's take a flight,
In this whimsical, moonlit night!

Starry Whispers Beneath the Sky

Stars play hide and seek, what a game,
The moon tells jokes, it's never the same.
The night's got jokes, they crack me up,
Even bats join in, they're quite the sup.

Fireflies dance, think they're all so bright,
They trip and fall, oh what a sight!
The owls hoot softly, but have a laugh,
Telling tall tales of their nightly path.

Clouds drift by, aren't they quite the team?
Shaping things like an artist's dream.
The night winks slyly, remember the show?
With all its antics, it steals the glow.

So let's grab popcorn, sit on the grass,
Watch nature's sitcom, oh what a class!
For every twinkling, there's a punchline,
In the vast theater where stars align.

The Golden Embrace of Dimming Light

Sunset whispers, 'What a crazy day!'
Birds squawk gossip, then fly away.
A cat snaps at shadows, plotting revenge,
While dogs just watch, they never will binge.

The sun makes faces, all puffy and red,
Trees start to shuffle, like they are fed.
Laughter erupts as squirrels take flight,
Chasing after dreams brought on by the light.

The horizon giggles, it's quite a tease,
Waving goodbye, but not with ease.
A warm hug lingers, we all feel it near,
As night casts shadows, the stars start to cheer.

Twilight pranks us, like it's got a plan,
To trick our senses, oh it's quite the span!
So here's to the dusk, full of snickers and glee,
A comedy show, beneath the old tree.

Crickets' Serenade in Dusk's Warmth

Crickets chirp tunes, quite out of tune,
They're like a band lost under the moon.
Their beat is a mix of zigzag and zany,
A serenade silly — oh how they sway me!

Frogs join the choir, but can't find their note,
While fireflies whirl, in their glitzy coat.
The ponds reflect laughter, echoing back,
As frogs leap and plop, weighing down the track.

The night air is thick with giggles and squeaks,
As critters parade in their funny peaks.
A raccoon steals snacks while the rest take flight,
Making a ruckus, oh what a sight!

So dance with the crickets, tap to the beat,
Under the laughter of night, we're complete.
With every chirp, forget all your woes,
For in this wild show, hilarity flows.

When Light Meets the Velvet Night

When day yawns widely, it's time for a snack,
The sun sneezes gold, and then it's a whack.
Clouds stretch and wiggle, it's joke time again,
As sunlight tiptoes, on silliness zen.

The horizon blushes, 'Oh don't look at me!'
It's like a first date, a sight to see.
Stars peek with laughter, a twinkle and wink,
Ready for mischief, they'll never rethink.

Another day's ended, let's dance with delight,
As shadows grow bold, it's their party night.
Each flicker of light, keeps the giggles near,
In the theater of darkness, there's much to cheer.

So hold onto your hats, as the dusk takes its bow,
The stars take the stage, oh how they know how!
In this cosmic fun, we all play a part,
With laughter so bright, it warms every heart.

Stars that Sing of Silent Tranquility

When clouds play hide and seek with stars,
The sky's a stage, with laughs from Mars.
A comet jokes, with a tail so long,
It twirls and swirls, like a dance so strong.

Moonbeams chuckle, casting shadows wide,
Whispers of laughter float on the tide.
Planets giggle in their merry round,
While stardust sprinkles joy all around.

In this cosmic circus, oh what a show,
The universe jests with a gleeful glow.
Nebulas burst into fits of cheer,
As twinkling lights bring smiles we hold dear.

So raise a glass to the night so bright,
Where humor thrives in celestial light.
Let's dance with stardust, high up in the air,
For laughter exists, everywhere, I swear!

The Dance of Shadows and Gleams

With shadows waltzing in moonlight's glow,
The trees tell tales, as breezes blow.
Dancing like socks that lost their pair,
The ground chuckles; it's no time to care.

A mouse in a tuxedo finds his stance,
While fireflies join in a glowing prance.
Each flicker of light, a giggle in the air,
As laughter echoes from everywhere.

The owls hoot jokes from their lofty sight,
While crickets chirp with all their might.
In this vibrant scene, the silly unfolds,
A symphony of chuckles, a story retold.

So sway to the rhythm, let your worries drift,
In this night of whims, let laughter be your gift.
For each shadow's sway, and each silvery gleam,
Is a step in the dance of a glorious dream!

Warm Embrace of the Cosmic Breeze

A gentle breeze brings whispers and sighs,
Tickling the leaves, oh, how they surprise!
Stars twinkle in rhythm, like a banjo's twang,
As the night plays on, the universe sang.

The wind starts to giggle, tickles my nose,
While the moon wears a smile, in grandiose pose.
Clouds puff up cheerfully, just like a cat,
As they lounge and stretch, imagine that!

In this comical realm where the absurd reigns,
The cosmos joins in with joy that remains.
While planets discuss their latest blunder,
The night is alive with enchanting wonder.

So dance with the breeze, let your spirit flow,
In the warm embrace, where silliness grows.
For each happy gust brings a story so bright,
A playful adventure in the heart of the night!

Mercurial Moments in the Gloaming

In the fading light, as day waves goodbye,
A squirrel in a hat gives a wink from on high.
The sun bows down, with a cheeky grin,
While fireflies gather, it's time to begin.

Casting shadows like puppets on strings,
The sky turns to canvas where imagination springs.
A jester named Jupiter trips on a star,
And laughs echo wide, oh, how bizarre!

With giggles of breezes through branches they weave,
The night brings forth joy, oh, we shan't leave!
For every minute's a riddle in time,
A cryptic charade, like a nursery rhyme.

So let us embrace these mercurial sights,
Join laughter and whimsy in twinkling nights.
As moments unfold in this delightful dream,
We find joy in the mystery, as silly as it seems!

Luminous Moments: A Nighttime Reverie

Once I tried to chase the moon,
But tripped on my old broom.
The stars all giggled on their way,
While I just sat there, lost in play.

Fireflies joined the dance with glee,
Whispering secrets just for me.
I offered them some cheese and bread,
They blinked and flew away instead.

My cat considered a nighttime spree,
Prowling about, so wild and free.
She found a shadow, gave a fright,
Turns out it was just a sleeping kite.

Laughter echoed through the trees,
As friends recounted silly pleas.
A night of joy, a sparkly jest,
Under a glow, we felt so blessed.

Serenity's Canvas of Illuminated Nights

Under a sky of vast delight,
I painted dreams with twinkling light.
A squirrel stole my picnic snacks,
He laughed and vanished with some cracks.

Moonbeams shone upon my hat,
While a raccoon danced near my mat.
I tossed him crumbs in playful jest,
He winked and claimed he was the best.

The breeze sang songs with gentle cheer,
As owls watched with a curious leer.
They hooted tunes that made me grin,
As fireflies joined the nightly din.

In this vast, playful, painted space,
I twirled around in sheer embrace.
The canvas glows with quirky sights,
As I savor these playful nights.

A Palette of Peace in Celestial Shades.

Stars flicker like the faulted lights,
While clouds play peek-a-boo in flights.
I spilled my drink while trying to toast,
With giggles rising, I made a boast.

Night critters buzz and hum about,
As I share secrets with a pout.
They stole the show, my words turned shy,
As someone's dog dashed past the sky.

Painting dreams with a laughter brush,
I mixed my joys in a fancied rush.
As the moon winked down, what a scene!
With colors sprouted from the unseen.

In this palette of shadows, I swear,
Life's a canvas, quirky, rare.
I made this night a playful game,
Under a sky that called my name.

Dancing Under Starlit Skies

With twinkling stars just overhead,
I tried to dance but slipped instead.
My friends all chuckled at my fall,
As I declared, 'I meant that call!'

The moonlight blinked with a cheeky grin,
While my dog joined in with a spin.
He chased his tail with much delight,
As shadows played in the cool night.

A troupe of crickets found their groove,
Their symphony was hard to move.
We clapped along, in silly stance,
And fell into a jolly dance.

So here we sway beneath the skies,
With laughter echoing our cries.
In the dance of dusk, we find our way,
Where playful spirits love to play.